# The 2030 Prophecy

The 2030 Prophecy

# The 2030 Prophecy

**Steve Hanks**

The 2030 Prophecy

The 2030 Prophecy

ISBN: 979-8-9878999-6-0

First paperback edition February 2026

The 2030 Prophecy

# Acknowledgements

This book would not exist without the extraordinary research presented in the *Messiah 2030* video series on YouTube. I am deeply grateful to the creators for their rigorous scholarship and for making it freely available.

Any errors in interpretation or application are entirely my own.

# Table of Contents

The 2030 Prophecy

## CHAPTER ONE

# The Day and Hour No Man Knows

Every time someone starts talking about biblical prophecy and end-times timelines, somebody in the room pulls out their trump card:

*"But no one knows the day or the hour!"*

And just like that, the conversation is over. Case closed. Go home. Stop looking at calendars.

Here's the problem: the people quoting that verse have no idea what it actually means. They've turned a first-century Jewish IDIOM into a theological shutdown button. And in doing so, they've ignored the very context Jesus was speaking in and contradicted multiple other scriptures in the process.

Let's fix that.

## The Verse in Question

"But about that day and hour no one knows, not even the angels of heaven, nor the son, but the father only" (Matthew 24:36).

There it is. The verse that's been weaponized to shut down prophetic inquiry for centuries. But before we accept the standard interpretation, let's ask a few questions that most people never bother to ask.

## What Does "About" Mean?

The Greek word translated "about" is *peri* (περί). It's a preposition meaning "concerning," "regarding," or "about." It introduces the topic of discussion.

So Jesus is saying: "*Concerning* that day and hour, no one knows...*"

He's introducing a topic. He's not making an absolute prohibition on ever knowing. He's making a statement about the current state of knowledge at that moment, and there's a very specific reason why.

## The Feast "No Man Knows"

Here's what your pastor probably never told you: "The day and hour no man knows" was a common Jewish **idiom** for a specific feast. *Yom Teruah*, the Feast of Trumpets.

An idiom is slang. It's like saying "it's raining cats and dogs." Nobody thinks puppy dogs and kitty cats are falling from the sky. It's an expression. Everybody in that culture knows exactly what it means. First-century Jews hearing "the day no man knows" didn't scratch their heads wondering what Jesus meant. They knew. He was talking about THE FEAST OF TRUMPETS.

Why? Because the Feast of Trumpets is the only feast that falls on the first day of a Hebrew month. (Now pay attention carefully.) Hebrew months begin with the new moon. And the new moon had to be visually confirmed by two witnesses before the Sanhedrin could officially declare the month had begun.

Picture this: Two men stand on a hilltop outside Jerusalem, scanning the western horizon at sunset. They're looking for the first sliver of the new moon. The moment they see it, they sprint to the

Sanhedrin. They testify. The Sanhedrin examines them. And if their testimony is credible, the shofar blasts and the new month is declared. Remember that word: DECLARED.

This created a 48-hour window of uncertainty. The feast would fall on one of two possible days, and nobody knew which one until the witnesses confirmed it.

So when first-century Jews talked about "the day no man knows," they weren't speaking philosophically about the unknowability of the future. They were talking about a specific feast with a specific calendrical quirk.

Jesus wasn't shutting down prophetic inquiry. *He was identifying the exact feast he was talking about.*

And here's where it gets interesting. If Jesus used this idiom to identify the Feast of Trumpets, what was he actually telling them? He wasn't saying "you'll never figure it out." He was saying "I'm returning on the Feast of Trumpets." The very phrase that's been used to shut down prophetic inquiry for centuries is actually a clue pointing to the exact feast of his return.

He told them which feast. In plain sight. And for 2,000 years, most have missed it.

### So Why Say "Watch"?

If Jesus meant "you can never know, so don't bother looking," why did he immediately follow up with this?

"Watch therefore, for you do not know what hour your Lord is coming" (Matthew 24:42).

Wait. If we can *never* know, why watch? You don't watch for something you believe is fundamentally unknowable. You watch for something you expect to be able to recognize when it's approaching.

The Greek word for "watch" is *grēgoreō* (γρηγορέω). It means to stay awake, to be vigilant, to be alert. It's an active word. It implies expectation. It implies that watching will produce results.

You don't tell someone to watch for a bus that will never come. You tell them to watch because the bus *is* coming, and you don't want them to miss it.

Now then, you'd better buckle up here, because this'll send you into the ionosphere. What does WATCHING look like? It's not passive. It's not sitting on your porch staring at the sky. Watching includes STUDYING. It means digging into Daniel. Working out the timelines. Examining the feast calendar. Doing the math.

In fact, would you like to know if you're "watching"? You're doing it right now. Studying this book. You are in preparation by studying. THAT'S watching. This is what Jesus commanded.

### Paul Settles the Debate

If there's any doubt about whether believers can know the timing, Paul eliminates it in 1 Thessalonians 5: "But concerning the times and the seasons, brethren, you have no need that I should write to you. For you yourselves know perfectly that the day of the Lord so comes as a thief in the night...**But you, brethren, are not in darkness, so that this Day should overtake you as a thief**" (1 Thessalonians 5:1-2, 4).

Read that again. Slowly.

"You are not in darkness." "This Day should NOT overtake you as a thief."

How does a thief catch you off guard? By showing up when you don't expect him. You didn't know he was coming. So if Paul says that day will NOT overtake you as a thief, what's he saying?

There's only one way to not be overtaken as a thief in the night. **You know when he's coming.**

You can certainly be "overtaken" by something you're clueless about. The very promise that it won't surprise you means you have the ability to see it approaching. Paul isn't giving you a nice sentiment. He's stating a fact about your capacity to know.

"You yourselves know perfectly." That's not ambiguity. That's confidence. Paul expected believers to understand the times and seasons well enough to not be caught off guard. How do we know the times and the seasons? By STUDYING. Congratulations! By the time you finish this book…YOU'LL KNOW.

If you can't know, Paul's entire argument collapses. "It won't overtake you as a thief" would be meaningless if there's no way to see it coming.

But Paul meant exactly what he said. You can know. You should know. And if you're paying attention to the signs, the seasons, the prophetic calendar, **you will know**.

### The Greek Word for "Knows"

Let's go deeper. The Greek word translated "knows" in Matthew 24:36 is *oida* (οἶδα). When Jesus says "only the father KNOWS," this word doesn't just mean "to have information." It carries a sense of authoritative declaration. The kind of authority that gives you the right to announce something officially. It's a DECLARATION.

Think about the two witnesses watching for the new moon. They might see the moon. They might know they saw it. But they don't have the authority to declare the new month. Only the Sanhedrin had that authority. Only the father has the authority to declare "now."

Jesus isn't saying "nobody has any clue." He's saying "nobody has the authority to make the official DECLARATION except the father." There's a massive difference between not knowing something exists and not having the authority to announce it. No one has the authority to announce his return. Only the father, which includes the Messiah who is the father clothed in a flesh body.

But I digress (as you'll see in a moment).

A wedding guest might know the wedding is about to start. But they don't *oida* it. They don't **declare** when the wedding starts. They don't have the authority to declare "the bride is coming." That's the father of the bride's job.

## But Wait...The Son Didn't Know?

This trips people up. If Jesus is God, how could he not know something?

He never said he didn't know. He said "only the father." And here's what most miss: Jesus IS one of the multitude of aspects of the father clothed in flesh. Which of the multitude of characteristics of the father? The word. Christ is THE WORD with a flesh body. "I and the father are one" wasn't metaphor. It was literal. When he said "only the father," he wasn't excluding himself. *He was identifying himself.*

Now let's go back to the *oida* point. ***Oida* is about authority to declare.** The father declares. And Christ, who is the visible manifestation of the invisible God, wasn't claiming ignorance. *He was claiming the declaration.*

It's not a statement of ignorance.

It's a statement of jurisdiction

## What About the Angels?

"Not even the angels of heaven..."

The Greek word is *angeloi (ἄγγελοι),* which simply means "messengers." In Hebrew, the equivalent is *malakim.* And here's something most people miss: *malakim* doesn't exclusively refer to heavenly beings. It's used throughout the Old Testament to describe human messengers, including prophets.

"Behold, I send my messenger" (Malachi 3:1). The word is *malak.* This refers to John the Baptist. A human prophet.

So when Jesus says "not even the *angeloi,*" he could be including both heavenly messengers and prophetic voices. **At that moment, neither celestial beings nor human prophets had the authority to declare the timing.** The father alone held that prerogative. And again, Jesus wasn't excluded from that knowledge. He **included** himself when he said, "Only the father knows." Never heard of that one to explain 'only the father knows,' did you!

## Daniel Was Told to Seal It. Until When?

"But you, Daniel, shut up the words, and seal the book until the time of the end. Many shall run to and fro, and knowledge shall increase" (Daniel 12:4).

17

"Go your way, Daniel, for the words are closed up and sealed till the time of the end" (Daniel 12:9).

The prophecy was sealed. But it wasn't sealed forever. It was sealed until a specific time. And that time? *"The time of the end."*

Raise your hand if you sense we're at "the time of the end."

If we're approaching that time (and the convergence of prophetic timelines suggests we are) then the seal is being broken. The knowledge that was hidden is becoming available. The patterns that were obscured are becoming visible.

"Many shall run to and fro, and knowledge shall increase." Sound familiar? We live in an age of unprecedented access to information. AI has more knowledge than all humans combined. Ancient manuscripts. Hebrew and Greek lexicons. Astronomical data. Calendrical calculations. All available at the click of a button.

The seal is lifting. And those who are watching, those not in darkness, are beginning to see what was hidden for generations.

### So Can We Know?

Let's recap:

"The day and hour no man knows" was a Jewish idiom for the Feast of Trumpets. The feast with a 48-hour uncertainty window due to moon-sighting requirements. Jesus wasn't hiding the timing. He was revealing it. He told us which feast he's returning on. Now we just need to determine which year. Stick with me. We're getting there.

Jesus commanded us to "watch," an active verb that implies that watching, which includes studying, produces results.

Paul explicitly said the Day of the Lord will not overtake believers as a thief because we are "not in darkness."

The Greek word *oida* implies *authority to declare,* not mere awareness.

Daniel's prophecy was sealed "until the time of the end." Not forever.

So yes. We can know. We WILL know.

We don't have the authority to declare. That remains the father's prerogative. But we have enough clarity to watch intelligently, to recognize the signs, to understand the seasons, and to not be caught off guard like the rest of the world.

The question isn't whether we can know.

The question is whether we're willing to look.

Turn the page. Let's start looking.

The 2030 Prophecy

## CHAPTER TWO

# When Did Herod Die?

You want to know when he's coming back? First we gotta know when he showed up the first time. And that starts with a dead king.

Matthew's gospel is crystal clear. Jesus was born while Herod was still breathing. So if we know when Herod croaked, we know Jesus was born before that. Simple, right?

You'd think. But scholars love to complicate things.

### The Two Camps

There's a debate in academic circles about when Herod died. Most historians say 4 BC. A smaller group insists it was 1 BC. Both sides agree on one thing: there was a lunar eclipse shortly before Herod's death, and he died before Passover.

The question is...which eclipse? Which Passover?

Here's where it gets interesting.

The 4 BC eclipse happened about 29 days before Passover. The 1 BC eclipse happened about 89 days before Passover.

The 1 BC crowd has one main argument: "29 days isn't enough time to get everything done between Herod's death and Passover." They've written long, complicated papers about funeral customs, travel times, and mourning periods. Very impressive. Very scholarly.

Very wrong.

## The Rushed Behavior Problem

See, the 1 BC people have a problem they can't solve.

Think about what had to happen after Herod died. Funerals, mourning periods, political negotiations, travel to Rome for imperial approval, security arrangements for the biggest festival of the year...the kind of stuff that takes months to sort out properly. That's their argument. And on paper, it sounds reasonable.

But Josephus, the Jewish historian who documented all of this, recorded what actually happened after Herod died. And what he recorded doesn't look like people who had 89 days to figure things out.

It looks like panic.

Archelaus, Herod's son and successor, immediately rubber-stamped all his father's military appointments. No review. No vetting. Just "yeah, you're all confirmed." That's not the behavior of someone with three months to spare. That's the behavior of someone who needs allies fast because Passover is coming and he's got problems.

The crowds started demanding tax relief and prisoner releases during the mourning period. During the funeral proceedings. They didn't wait politely until the grieving was over. Why not? Because they knew time was running out before the big festival. Everyone would be in Jerusalem for Passover, and if grievances weren't addressed by then, there'd be hell to pay.

Multiple heirs...Archelaus, Antipas, Salome...all raced to Rome simultaneously to get Augustus to confirm their inheritances. They didn't coordinate. They didn't take turns. They scrambled over each other like crabs in a bucket. Every single day mattered.

And then there's the massacre.

### 3,000 Dead Jews

Both the 4 BC and 1 BC camps acknowledge this happened. At Passover, right after Herod's death, Archelaus ordered the slaughter of 3,000 Jewish worshipers in the temple precincts. It was so catastrophic that Passover was cancelled. First time in history.

Now here's the question the 1 BC scholars can't answer:

Why?

If Archelaus had 89 days to consolidate power, why did everything explode into mass murder? Three months is plenty of time to negotiate with religious leaders, address grievances, prepare proper security, defuse tensions. You don't massacre 3,000 people at your first Passover as king if you had a full quarter of a year to get your house in order.

But you might if you only had 29 days.

Twenty-nine days to bury your father with proper honors. Twenty-nine days to secure your claim to the throne. Twenty-nine days to handle a population that hated your family. Twenty-nine days before a million pilgrims flood into Jerusalem expecting everything to run smoothly.

The massacre makes no sense with 89 days. It makes perfect sense with 29. The chaos itself proves the timeline.

## "Just Before Passover"

Josephus himself says Herod died "just before" Passover.

Let me ask you something. If someone died three months before Christmas, would you say they died "just before Christmas"? Of course not. That's not "just before." That's a different season entirely.

29 days is "just before."

89 days is not.

Josephus wasn't sloppy with his words. He was a trained historian writing for a Roman audience that expected precision. He said what he meant. Herod died just before Passover, and there's only one eclipse that fits that description.

## The Josephus Math

Josephus gives us two independent markers for Herod's reign.

First, Herod died 37 years after the Roman Senate appointed him king in 40 BC. 40 BC. Count forward 37 years. 40... 39... 38... you get the idea. When you hit 37 years, you're at 4 BC. Remember, there's no year zero. You go straight from 1 BC to 1 AD.

Now the second one. Herod conquered Jerusalem in 37 BC. Josephus says he died 34 years later. 37 BC plus 34 years. Same destination. 4 BC.

Two different starting points. Two different counts. Same answer. That's not coincidence. That's confirmation.

But wait. There's more.

## Antipater's Trial

Antipater was Herod's son. The one who schemed to have his half-brothers executed so he could inherit the throne. Real piece of work, this guy. Poisoned his father's mind against the competition, watched them die, then made his move for the crown.

But eventually his own plot to murder Herod was discovered, and he was put on trial before Varus, the Roman governor of Syria.

Here's the thing. Varus's governorship is independently documented through Roman records and coins. We don't have to guess when he served. He governed Syria from 6 to 4 BC. And multiple sources place Antipater's trial in 5 BC.

**That's not calculated backward from Herod's death. That's anchored to Roman administrative records that have nothing to do with biblical chronology.**

Antipater was tried in 5 BC. He was executed five days before Herod died. And Herod died shortly before Passover.

The 4 BC timeline fits like a glove. The 1 BC timeline requires you to ignore the trial date entirely, pretend the Roman records don't exist, and hope nobody notices.

## The Bottom Line

The 1 BC advocates have built elaborate theories based on eclipse calculations and manuscript debates. They've written dissertations and done the astronomy. Very impressive work, honestly.

But they can't explain why 3,000 people died at Passover if Archelaus had three months to prevent it.

They can't explain why everyone was rushing if they had 89 days.

They can't explain why Josephus said "just before" when he supposedly meant "almost three months."

And they can't explain Antipater's trial being documented in 5 BC.

Sometimes scholars get so lost in complicated theories that they miss what's obvious to anyone with common sense. The 4 BC date isn't defended by elaborate arguments. It's proven by the chaos. The rush. The massacre. The behavior of people who knew Passover was coming and didn't have time to fix what was broken.

Herod died in the spring of 4 BC. Which means Jesus was born before that.

Which means we now have our anchor point.

## CHAPTER THREE

# The Ministry Timeline

Herod died in the spring of 4 BC. Jesus was born before that. Which puts his birth in 5 BC at the earliest.

But can we get more specific?

There's good reason to believe he was born on the Feast of Tabernacles...late September, 5 BC. The priestly schedule, the six-month gap between John's conception and Mary's, the gestation math. It all points to Tabernacles. And John's gospel says the Word became flesh and "dwelt" among us. That Greek word is eskēnōsen. It literally means "pitched his tent" or "tabernacled."

If Jesus was born on the Feast of Tabernacles, John wasn't being poetic. He was being precise.

September 27, 5 BC. Feast of Tabernacles. That's our working date.

Why does this matter? Because if we know when he was born, we can figure out when he started his ministry. And if we know when he started, we can figure out when he died. And if we know when he died...well, that's where things get interesting.

One piece at a time. Let's keep moving.

## The 15th Year of Tiberius

Luke tells us that John the Baptist began his ministry "in the fifteenth year of the reign of Tiberius Caesar." That's our anchor for when everything kicked off.

But here's where people get confused. Tertullian, an early church father, said the Messiah was anointed in the 12th year of Tiberius. Luke says the 15th. Eusebius, the church historian, said the Messiah suffered in the 19th year of Tiberius.

Are they contradicting each other?

Nope. They're just counting differently.

Think of it like a family business.

Say your dad owns a company. You start working there at 16, learning the ropes, making decisions, basically running things alongside him. By the time you're 20, you're doing most of the work. Then dad dies when you're 22, and now you're officially the boss.

Here's the question: when did you start running the company?

Your employees might say you took over at 22. That's when your name went on the door. But your mom says you've been running it since you were 16. She watched you do it.

Who's right? Both of them. They're just counting differently.

Same thing with Tiberius. He started co-ruling with Augustus around 12 CE. Did the work, commanded the armies, made the calls. But Augustus didn't die until 14 CE. That's when Tiberius officially became emperor.

So when ancient historians say "the 12th year of Tiberius" or "the 15th year of Tiberius," they might be counting from different starting lines. One counts from when he started doing the job. The other counts from when he got the title.

Here's what matters: when you do the math from either starting point, you land in the same place. Around 26 CE. Luke, Tertullian, and Eusebius aren't disagreeing. They're confirming each other without realizing it.

Different starting points. Same destination.

### The Temple Confirmation

John's gospel gives us independent confirmation from a completely different angle.

During Jesus's first Passover of his ministry, the Jewish leaders said to him, "It has taken forty-six years to build this temple, and you will raise it in three days?"

Forty-six years.

We know from historical records that Herod began major reconstruction of the temple in 20 BC. Forty-six years of construction brings us to 26 CE.

This wasn't the first Passover after his baptism by accident. This was 27 CE. Which means his ministry launched in the fall of 26 CE. Which means Luke, Tertullian, and the temple construction timeline all point to the same window.

Three independent witnesses. Same date.

## About Thirty Years Old

Luke says Jesus was "about thirty years of age" when he began his ministry.

Some people read that as vague. Like Luke was guessing. "I don't know, somewhere around thirty, give or take."

That's not what's happening here.

When someone tells you they're "about thirty," they're not 45. They're not 22. They're close. Maybe 29. Maybe just turned 30. But they're in the neighborhood.

Here's what makes this interesting.

If Jesus was born on the Feast of Tabernacles...that's Tishrei 15 on the Hebrew calendar. Late September.

If he began his ministry on the Day of Atonement...that's Tishrei 10. Five days before Tabernacles.

You see what that means?

He started his ministry five days before his 30th birthday.

Luke wasn't being vague. He was being precise. "About thirty" is exactly right when you're five days short of the mark.

## Why Yom Kippur?

The Day of Atonement wasn't a random start date.

This is the holiest day on the Hebrew calendar. The one day each year when the high priest entered the Holy of Holies to make atonement for Israel. The day that pointed forward to the ultimate sacrifice. The day that foreshadowed everything Jesus came to do.

And there's a practical reason too. Numbers 4:3 says priests began their service at age 30. Jesus couldn't officially begin his public ministry until he met the age requirement. Five days early, but "about thirty" gets the job done.

He launched his ministry on the Day of Atonement, at the threshold of the required age, in the year that multiple independent sources confirm.

This isn't coincidence. This is choreography.

### The First Passover

So his ministry starts in the fall of 26 CE. His first Passover comes in the spring of 27 CE. That's when the forty-six years conversation happens in John chapter 2.

Why does this matter?

Because it establishes the length of his ministry. From fall 26 CE to spring 30 CE gives us roughly three and a half years. One Passover in 27. Another in 28. Another in 29. And then the final one in 30.

The Passover when he became the Passover Lamb.

We're building something here. Each piece locks into the next. Born Tabernacles 5 BC. Ministry launched Yom Kippur 26 CE. First Passover 27 CE. Final Passover...

But hold on. Didn't he die in 33 CE? That's what you've always heard, right?

Yeah. About that.

## CHAPTER FOUR

# The Crucifixion Date

We've established his birth. We've established when his ministry began. Now we need to nail down when it ended.

Or more precisely...when something else began.

### The Math

If Jesus started his ministry in the fall of 26 CE, and his ministry lasted roughly three and a half years, that brings us to the spring of 30 CE.

Simple addition. Nothing fancy.

But let's confirm it from multiple angles. Because when independent witnesses point to the same date, you're not dealing with coincidence. You're dealing with fact.

### John's Passovers

The gospel of John records multiple Passovers during Jesus's ministry.

The first one is in John chapter 2. That's the forty-six years conversation we already covered. Passover, 27 CE.

There's another feast mentioned in John 5, which many scholars identify as Passover. That's 28 CE.

John 6 explicitly mentions Passover. That's 29 CE.

And then the final Passover. The one where he became the Lamb. John 13 through 19. That's 30 CE.

Four Passovers. A ministry spanning from fall 26 CE to spring 30 CE. Three and a half years.

## Eusebius Confirms

Remember Eusebius? The church historian who said the Messiah suffered in the 19th year of Tiberius?

Let's do the math again.

If you count from Tiberius's co-regency starting in 12 CE, the 19th year brings you to 30 or 31 CE. Account for how ancient historians handled partial years, and you land at 30 CE.

Eusebius didn't know he was confirming the same date Luke and Tertullian pointed to for the ministry start. He was just recording what he knew. But all these independent sources keep landing in the same spot.

That's not an accident.

## Wednesday, April 5

Here's something that might surprise you.

Jesus wasn't crucified on Friday.

I know. "Good Friday" is what you've heard your whole life. But think about it for a second. Jesus said he'd be in the heart of the earth for three days and three nights. That's what he told the Pharisees when they asked for a sign. "As Jonah was three days and three nights in the belly of the great fish, so will the Son of Man be three days and three nights in the heart of the earth."

Three days. Three nights.

Friday afternoon to Sunday morning doesn't give you that. Count it yourself. Friday night. Saturday day. Saturday night. That's one full day and two nights. Maybe you can stretch it to two days if you're being generous. But three days and three nights? The math doesn't work.

So why do people say Friday? Because the gospels say he was buried before the sabbath. They assume that means Saturday, the weekly sabbath. But that week had two sabbaths. Passover is a high sabbath, no matter what day it falls on. That year it fell on Thursday.

So Thursday was the Passover sabbath. Saturday was the weekly sabbath. And Friday? Friday was a regular day. That's when the women prepared their spices.

Wednesday works.

Wednesday afternoon, in the tomb before sundown. Wednesday evening is the beginning of the High Sabbath, Passover. Wednesday evening to Thursday evening, the High Sabbath is the first day.

Thursday evening to Friday evening. Friday is a regular workday when the ladies prepared the spices. The second day.

Friday evening starts the weekly sabbath. Friday evening to Saturday evening is the weekly sabbath, the third day.

Three nights. Three days. He rises sometime after sundown Saturday, which on the Hebrew calendar is already the start of Sunday, the first day of the week.

Died on Passover. In the grave during the Feast of Unleavened Bread. Raised from the dead on First Fruits. The feast celebrates the first harvest. Jesus is the first one raised from the dead, the firstborn among many brethren.

Wednesday, April 5, 30 CE. That's when he died.

Sunday, April 8, 30 CE. That's when he rose.

## Why This Matters

I could end this chapter here. We've established the date. Case closed. Let's move on.

But I'm not going to do that. Because this date isn't just a historical marker. It's not trivia for bible nerds who like arguing about calendars.

Something started on First Fruits, 30 CE.

Something most Christians have never heard of. Something that's been ticking for almost two thousand years. Two ancient clocks, buried in the prophets, counting down to the same destination.

One for Israel. One for Judah.

Both ending at the same place. The same year. The same feast.

You're about to find out what's been running in the background this whole time.

## CHAPTER FIVE

# The Punishment of Israel

Around 593 BC, God told the prophet Ezekiel to do something strange.

He told him to lie on his left side for 390 days. One day for each year of Israel's punishment. Then lie on his right side for 40 days. One day for each year of Judah's punishment.

Left side faced north. That's where Israel was. Right side faced south. That's where Judah was. Two kingdoms. Two punishment periods. Two separate clocks.

But before Ezekiel started lying down, God told him to do something else. Build a model of Jerusalem on a clay tablet. Set up miniature siege works around it. Battering rams. Ramps. Enemy camps. Act out a siege against the city.

And then place an iron plate between yourself and the city.

That iron plate is the key to everything.

### The Iron Plate

What does an iron plate between the attacker and the city represent?

A failed siege. A barrier. Something that stops the attack from succeeding.

And that points us to a specific moment in history.

701 BC. Sennacherib, king of Assyria, surrounded Jerusalem with his army. This was the most powerful military force on earth. City after city had fallen to them. Now they had Jerusalem in their sights.

But Jerusalem didn't fall.

According to 2 Kings 19, God sent an angel that killed 185,000 Assyrian soldiers in a single night. Sennacherib packed up and went home. The siege failed. **The iron plate held.**

That's the event Ezekiel was pointing to. The first siege of Jerusalem. The unsuccessful one. And that's where Israel's punishment clock starts ticking.

701 BC.

## The 390 Years

God assigned Israel 390 years of punishment. Starting from 701 BC, count forward 390 years.

701 BC plus 390 years brings you to 311 BC.

Did Israel repent by 311 BC? No. They were scattered. The northern kingdom had been conquered by Assyria long before. The people were dispersed among the nations. No repentance. No return to God.

So what happens when Israel doesn't repent after the assigned punishment period?

Leviticus 26 tells us.

## The Sevenfold Multiplication

Leviticus 26 lays out a series of warnings. If Israel disobeys, God will punish them. If they still don't repent, he'll increase the punishment sevenfold. The Hebrew word is sheva. Seven times.

This isn't just a metaphor for "a lot." It's a specific multiplier. Seven times the original punishment.

Israel didn't repent after 390 years. So the punishment gets multiplied.

390 times 7 equals 2,730 years.

Now we're not counting from 311 BC. We're counting the full 2,730 years from the original starting point. From the iron plate. From the failed siege.

701 BC plus 2,730 years.

Do the math. Account for the fact that there's no year zero between 1 BC and 1 AD. And you land in the year 2030.

Israel's punishment period expires in 2030.

## But Wait

You might be thinking, okay, that's interesting math. But it's just one calculation. Could be coincidence. Could be someone working backward from a date they wanted to land on and finding numbers that fit.

Fair enough.

So let's look at Judah.

DID THAT JUST HAPPEN?

You just watched 2,730 years of prophetic math land on a single year. 2030.

And we're not done.

I built a single printable page called The Timeline — every date, every calculation, every prophetic clock from this book laid out on one sheet. Stick it on your fridge. Bring it to Bible study. Hand it to the guy who says "no man knows the day or the hour."

Here's how to get it:

1. Go to ShittyToHappy.com/timeline

2. Enter your email

3. Hit the button

No password. No hoops. The Timeline is yours instantly.

ShittyToHappy.com/timeline

CHAPTER SIX

# The Punishment of Judah

Now let's look at the other side of Ezekiel's prophecy.

When he lay on his right side facing south, he represented Judah. Forty days. One day for each year of their punishment.

But Judah's clock doesn't start in 701 BC. Judah's clock starts much later.

### The 40-Year Warning

When Jesus was crucified on Passover, 30 CE, something shifted. The veil in the temple tore from top to bottom. The sacrificial system was complete. What it foreshadowed had arrived.

But God didn't immediately destroy the temple. He gave Judah forty years to repent. Forty years to recognize what had happened. Forty years of warning signs so obvious, so supernatural, that nobody could miss them.

The Talmud records what happened during those forty years. And it's terrifying.

The lot for the Lord, which was supposed to randomly appear in either the high priest's right hand or left hand, started showing up in the left hand every single time. For forty straight years. The odds of that happening by chance are astronomical.

The westernmost lamp of the menorah refused to stay lit. Priests would fill it with oil, trim the wick, do everything right. It would go out anyway. For forty years.

The massive temple doors, so heavy it took twenty men to move them, started swinging open by themselves. Every night. For forty years. The rabbis saw this as an omen that the temple was preparing to let in its enemies.

And the crimson thread stopped turning white.

Every year on the Day of Atonement, a crimson thread was tied to the scapegoat. If God accepted the sacrifice, the thread would miraculously turn white. Isaiah 1:18... "Though your sins are like scarlet, they shall be as white as snow."

For forty years, the thread stayed red.

God was shouting. Judah wasn't listening.

## 70 CE

In the year 70, the Romans surrounded Jerusalem. This time there was no iron plate. No angelic army to wipe out the attackers overnight. The siege succeeded. The temple burned. The people were scattered.

Judah's forty-year warning period was over. They hadn't repented. Now the punishment clock started ticking.

## The Double Multiplication

Here's where Judah's calculation differs from Israel's.

Israel got one multiplication. 390 times 7 equals 2,730 years.

Judah gets two.

Forty years times 7 equals 280 years. That takes us from 70 CE to 350 CE.

Did Judah repent by 350 CE? No. By that point, Christianity had become the official religion of Rome. The Jewish people were scattered across the empire, persecuted, marginalized. No national repentance. No return to God.

So the punishment multiplies again.

280 times 7 equals 1,960 years.

Starting from 70 CE, go forward 1,960 years.

You land in 2030.

## The Convergence

Do you see what just happened?

Israel's punishment period: 701 BC plus 2,730 years equals 2030.

Judah's punishment period: 70 CE plus 1,960 years equals 2030.

Two different starting points. Two different calculations. Two different houses that split apart almost three thousand years ago.

Both clocks expire in the exact same year.

This has never happened before. And given the mathematics, it will never happen again. The convergence is a one-time event in human history.

2030 isn't a guess. It isn't speculation. It isn't someone picking a date and working backward to make the numbers fit.

It's where the math lands when you let scripture do the talking.

But here's the question that should be forming in your mind right about now. If both punishment periods end in 2030, what happens between now and then? Is there a trigger? A starting gun? A specific event that kicks off the final countdown?

There is.

And Daniel told us exactly when it would happen.

CHAPTER SEVEN

# Daniel's 70 Weeks

Around 539 BC, while the Jewish people were still in Babylonian exile, the prophet Daniel received one of the most precise prophetic timelines in all of scripture.

Seventy weeks are determined for your people and for your holy city.

That's Daniel 9:24. And before we go any further, let's get one thing straight. These aren't literal weeks. The Hebrew word is shavua, which simply means "a unit of seven." Seven what? Context tells us. In this case, seven years.

Seventy units of seven years. That's 490 years total.

Daniel was told these 490 years would accomplish six specific things. Finish the transgression. Make an end of sins. Make reconciliation for iniquity. Bring in everlasting righteousness. Seal up vision and prophecy. Anoint the Most Holy.

The first three happened at the cross. The last three are still coming.

But here's what makes this prophecy remarkable. Daniel wasn't just told what would happen. He was told when.

## The Starting Point

Know therefore and understand, that from the going forth of the command to restore and build Jerusalem until Messiah the Prince, there shall be seven weeks and sixty-two weeks.

Seven plus sixty-two equals sixty-nine weeks. Sixty-nine times seven equals 483 years.

From the decree to restore Jerusalem until Messiah the Prince...483 years.

So when was the decree?

There were actually several decrees related to Jerusalem during this period. Cyrus issued one in 539 BC. Darius issued another around 520 BC. But both of those were about rebuilding the temple. Construction projects. Bricks and mortar.

Daniel's prophecy didn't say "rebuild." It said "restore."

That's a different word with a different meaning. Restore implies bringing something back to its former condition. Not just the buildings, but the city itself. Its government. Its legal authority. Its ability to function as a Jewish city under Jewish law.

That's exactly what Artaxerxes authorized in 458 BC.

Ezra 7 records the decree. It gave Ezra the authority to appoint judges and magistrates, to teach and enforce the Torah, and to punish anyone who refused to comply. We're talking fines, imprisonment, banishment, even death. This wasn't permission to stack stones. This was the restoration of Jewish self-governance.

Cyrus let them build a temple. Artaxerxes let them be a nation again.

458 BC is the decree that fits Daniel's language.

458 BC plus 483 years brings you to 26 CE.

That's exactly when Jesus began his ministry. The same date we established through Luke, Tertullian, and the temple construction timeline. Daniel called it five hundred years before it happened.

### The 70th Week Begins

So Messiah arrives right on schedule. Sixty-nine weeks fulfilled. One week remains.

The 70th week is a seven-year period. And according to Daniel 9:27, in the middle of that week, Messiah would bring an end to sacrifice and offering.

Middle of seven years. That's three and a half years.

Jesus's ministry lasted three and a half years. From fall 26 CE to spring 30 CE. Then he was "cut off, but not for himself." He died for others. And at the moment of his death, the veil in the temple tore. The sacrificial system was finished. Not because the priests stopped offering sacrifices. They kept that up for another forty years. But because the ultimate sacrifice had been made.

Messiah was cut off in the middle of Daniel's 70th week.

That leaves three and a half years unaccounted for.

### The Pause

This is where most people get lost. If the 70th week started when Jesus began his ministry, and he was cut off in the middle of it, where's the second half?

It hasn't happened yet.

The clock stopped on First Fruits, 30 CE. The day Jesus rose from the dead. Three and a half years of Daniel's prophecy remain unfulfilled. They're sitting there, waiting, like a paused movie.

Why the pause? Because God turned his attention to the nations. The times of the Gentiles began. The gospel went out to the whole world. And Israel's prophetic clock went silent.

But it won't stay silent forever.

## A Note on Alternative Calculations

Some scholars argue for a different starting point. They use Artaxerxes' second decree in 444 BC instead of 458 BC. To make their math work, they have to use "prophetic years" of 360 days instead of regular solar years.

Here's the problem with that.

Daniel used regular solar years everywhere else. When he talked about the seventy years of Babylonian captivity, he meant seventy actual years. Nobody suggests those were 360-day years. So why would he suddenly switch to a different calendar system for the 70-week prophecy?

He wouldn't.

The 444 BC calculation also lands you at 33 CE for the crucifixion. Which means Jesus's ministry would have to start around 29 or 30 CE. But we've already established from multiple independent sources that his ministry began in 26 CE. The 444 BC theory requires you to ignore Luke, Tertullian, Eusebius, and the temple construction timeline.

It's the same problem as the Friday crucifixion. People stretching the evidence to fit what they've always been taught instead of letting the evidence speak for itself.

458 BC. Solar years. Messiah arrives 26 CE. Cut off 30 CE. The math works without gymnastics.

### The Question

Daniel's 70th week paused in 30 CE with three and a half years remaining.

The punishment periods for Israel and Judah both expire in 2030.

That leaves an obvious question hanging in the air.

When does Daniel's clock start ticking again?

The 2030 Prophecy

CHAPTER EIGHT

# The Clock Restarts

Daniel's 70th week paused with three and a half years left on the clock.

The punishment periods for Israel and Judah both expire in 2030.

If you do the math backward from 2030, subtracting three and a half years, you land in the spring of 2027.

But we don't have to guess. Daniel told us exactly what would mark the restart.

### The Abomination of Desolation

In Daniel 9:27, right after describing how Messiah would be cut off in the middle of the week, Daniel mentions something called the "abomination of desolation." Jesus referenced it directly in Matthew 24:15. "When you see the abomination of desolation, spoken of by Daniel the prophet, standing in the holy place...then let those who are in Judea flee to the mountains."

This is the trigger event. The moment the abomination is set up, the final countdown begins.

### And here's a critical distinction.

*The abomination of desolation is not the tribulation. It's the event that triggers the tribulation. Think of it like a starting pistol at a race. The gunshot isn't the race. It's what starts the race. The abomination is the starting pistol. The three and a half years that follow — that's the tribulation.*

Daniel 12:11 gives us the exact number: "From the time that the daily sacrifice is taken away, and the abomination of desolation is set up, there shall be one thousand two hundred and ninety days."

1,290 days.

That's roughly three and a half years. The missing half of Daniel's 70th week.

## First Fruits 2027

Here's where it gets precise.

The clock stopped on First Fruits, 30 CE. The day Jesus rose from the dead. If God is consistent...and he always is...the clock restarts on the same feast it stopped on.

First Fruits 2027.

In 2027, First Fruits falls on March 27-28. Sundown March 27 to sundown March 28, to be exact.

That's when the abomination of desolation is set up. That's when Daniel's clock starts ticking again. That's when the final three and a half years begin.

## The Abomination of Desolation

The prophets saw what was coming. They didn't have words for it. No vocabulary for nuclear warheads, ICBMs, or radiation sickness. But they described what they saw as best they could.

Zechariah 14:12: "Their flesh shall dissolve while they stand on their feet, their eyes shall dissolve in their sockets, and their tongues shall dissolve in their mouths."

Flesh melting off the bones while people are still standing. Eyes liquefying. Tongues dissolving. That's not poetic language. That's a precise description of what happens in a nuclear blast. The heat hits so fast the body disintegrates before it can fall.

Zephaniah 1:18: "The whole land shall be devoured by the fire of his jealousy."

Isaiah 24:6: "Therefore the curse has devoured the earth, and those who dwell in it are desolate. Therefore the inhabitants of the earth are burned, and few men are left."

These prophets saw the end. They wrote down what they witnessed. We're the generation that finally has the technology to understand what they were describing.

Count forward 1,290 days from the beginning of the abomination of desolation starting on First Fruits 2027.

You land on Yom Kippur 2030. The Day of Atonement. October 6-7, 2030.

The same year both punishment periods expire. The same feast that marked the beginning of Jesus's ministry. Everything converges on a single point.

### The 1,260 Days

But wait. Daniel also mentions another number.

Revelation 11:3 says the two witnesses will prophesy for 1,260 days. Revelation 12:6 says the woman will be protected in the wilderness for 1,260 days.

1,290 days from the abomination to Yom Kippur.

1,260 days for the two witnesses.

What's the difference? Thirty days.

Both periods end on the same day...Yom Kippur 2030. But they start thirty days apart. The abomination is set up on First Fruits. Thirty days later, the two witnesses begin their ministry, and the woman flees to the wilderness.

Two countdowns. Two starting points. One finish line.

### The Two Witnesses

Thirty days after the abomination of desolation is set up, two men appear in Jerusalem.

We don't know their names. Revelation doesn't say. Some think it's Moses and Elijah. Some think Enoch and Elijah. It doesn't matter. What matters is what they do.

They prophesy. For 1,260 days. Three and a half years. Right in the middle of the chaos, right in the teeth of the beast's reign, two men stand in Jerusalem and speak the word of God without flinching.

And they are untouchable.

Revelation 11:5 says if anyone tries to harm them, fire comes out of their mouths and devours their enemies. Not figurative fire. Not symbolic fire. Fire. Anyone who tries to kill them dies the same way.

Think about that. For three and a half years, every assassination attempt fails. Every drone strike. Every sniper. Every military operation. Fire consumes them all. The most powerful governments on earth cannot silence two men standing on a street corner in Jerusalem.

But that's not all.

They have power to shut the sky so that no rain falls during the days of their prophecy. Three and a half years. No rain. Crops fail. Reservoirs dry up. Famine spreads. The world's economy collapses further. And everyone knows why. Those two men. Standing in Jerusalem. Untouchable.

They have power to turn water into blood. Rivers. Lakes. Reservoirs. Blood. Like Moses did in Egypt. Except this time it's global.

They have power to strike the earth with every kind of plague as often as they wish. Every plague. As often as they wish. Whenever they want. Whatever they want.

For 1,260 days, these two men are the most hated people on the planet. Every news network covers them. Every government wants them dead. Every person on earth knows their faces. And no one can do a thing about it.

Until the 1,260 days are complete.

### The Death

When they finish their testimony, the beast is allowed to kill them.

Not before. The moment their mission is complete, their protection lifts. And the beast rises from the abyss and murders them.

Their bodies fall in the street of Jerusalem. The great city. The city where their Lord was crucified.

And the world...celebrates.

Revelation 11:9-10 says the peoples and tribes and languages and nations will stare at their bodies for three and a half days and refuse to let them be buried. The whole world watches. Livestreamed. Broadcast. Everyone with a phone sees two dead bodies lying in a Jerusalem street.

And they rejoice.

They send gifts to one another. Like Christmas. Like a holiday. The two prophets who tormented the earth are finally dead. No more fire. No more drought. No more plagues. No more truth they didn't want to hear.

For three and a half days, the world throws a party over two corpses.

### The Resurrection

Then it happens.

Revelation 11:11. The breath of life from God enters them. They stand on their feet. And great fear falls on everyone who sees them.

The whole world is watching. Cameras are still rolling. The celebration stops mid-sentence. Because two dead men just stood up.

And then a loud voice from heaven says, "Come up here."

They ascend to heaven in a cloud. While their enemies watch.

In that same hour, a great earthquake strikes. A tenth of the city falls. Seven thousand people die. And the rest are terrified and give glory to the God of heaven.

Three and a half days from death to resurrection. Witnessed by the entire planet. Undeniable. Unexplainable. The God of Israel proving himself one more time.

### The Marker

And here's what no one is talking about.

Once the two witnesses appear in 2027, every single calculation in this book becomes undeniable. Not theory. Not speculation. Observable fact.

When two men show up in Jerusalem breathing fire and stopping rain, when the world watches and can't kill them no matter how hard they try, when the news networks can't explain what's happening...everyone will know.

The 1,260 days will be counting down in plain sight. You'll be able to mark your calendar. You'll be able to count the days. And when they finally fall, when the world celebrates for three and a half days, when they rise and ascend while the cameras roll...

There won't be a single person on planet earth who doubts the return of Messiah on the Feast of Trumpets, 2030.

This book will no longer be prophecy. It will be the news.

### The 1,335 Days

Daniel gives us one more number in chapter 12, verse 12: "Blessed is he who waits, and comes to the one thousand three hundred and thirty-five days."

1,335 days.

The two witnesses prophesy for 1,260 days. Add 75 days. You get 1,335.

Count forward 75 days from the end of the two witnesses' ministry.

You land in late December...right around Hanukkah. The Festival of Dedication. The Festival of Lights.

And here's something that should make the hair stand up on the back of your neck.

How old was Abraham when God cut the covenant with him?

Seventy-five years old. Genesis 12:4.

The blessing comes 75 days after the two witnesses complete their ministry. The Abrahamic covenant...the promise that through Abraham's seed all nations would be blessed...reaches its complete fulfillment at Hanukkah 2030.

The number that started the covenant journey is the number that finishes it.

And remember when Jesus was conceived? Six months after John, right around late December. Hanukkah. The Light of the World entered the world at the Festival of Lights.

Hanukkah bookends the whole story. His conception. The covenant's completion.

### The Timeline

Let me lay it out plain:

First Fruits 2027 (March 27-28): Abomination of desolation set up. Daniel's clock restarts. **1,290-day countdown begins.**

Thirty days later (late April 2027): Two witnesses begin prophesying. Woman flees to wilderness. **1,260-day countdown begins.**

Yom Kippur 2030 (October 6-7): Both countdowns end. Punishment periods for Israel and Judah expire. Daniel's 70th week complete. The 120th Jubilee.

Hanukkah 2030 (sunset, Friday December 20) 75 days after Yom Kippur. The blessing of Daniel 12:12. Abrahamic covenant fully realized.

Four independent timelines. All converging on the same eight-month window in 2030.

This isn't speculation. This is pattern recognition. God told us when. We just had to do the math.

The king is coming.

## EVERY CLOCK. ONE YEAR.

Israel's punishment: 2030. Judah's punishment: 2030. Daniel's 1,290 days: Yom Kippur 2030. The two witnesses' 1,260 days: Yom Kippur 2030. The 1,335-day blessing: Hanukkah 2030.

You just watched five independent timelines converge on the same eight-month window. That doesn't happen by accident. That happens by design.

I put every date, every calculation, and every prophetic clock from this book onto a single printable page called The Timeline.

Do this right now:

1. Go to ShittyToHappy.com/timeline

2. Enter your email

3. Hit the button

4. Download The Timeline instantly — no password required

Print it. Tape it to your wall. Start counting the days.

ShittyToHappy.com/timeline

CHAPTER NINE

# The Return

We've covered a lot of ground.

Herod died in 4 BC. Jesus was born on the Feast of Tabernacles in 5 BC. He began his ministry on the Day of Atonement in 26 CE, five days before his 30th birthday. He was crucified on Passover, Wednesday, April 5, 30 CE. He rose on First Fruits three days later.

Daniel's 70 weeks predicted the exact year of his arrival and the exact year of his death. The clock paused with three and a half years remaining.

The punishment period for Israel began in 701 BC. The punishment period for Judah began in 70 CE. Both expire in 2030.

Daniel's clock restarts on First Fruits 2027. The abomination of desolation is set up. The final three and a half years begin. The two witnesses prophesy for 1,260 days.

Every timeline we've traced points to the same destination.

Now let me show you what that day looks like.

## The Sky Splits

Revelation 6:14. "Then the sky receded as a scroll when it is rolled up."

Imagine standing outside. Maybe you're in your backyard. Maybe you're on a city street. Maybe you're on a mountaintop or a beach or stuck in traffic on the freeway. It doesn't matter where you are.

You look up.

And the sky peels back like a curtain.

Not clouds parting. Not a storm clearing. The sky itself rolling away like a scroll. The fabric of the heavens splitting open to reveal what's been hidden behind it all along.

Matthew 24:27. "For as the lightning comes from the east and flashes to the west, so also will the coming of the Son of Man be."

Lightning. Not a single bolt. Lightning that stretches from one horizon to the other. East to west. The entire sky on fire with light so bright it makes the sun look dim. So bright it blinds. So bright that every shadow on earth disappears in an instant.

This is not a quiet arrival.

This is not a gentle descent.

This is invasion.

Revelation 1:7. "Behold, he is coming with clouds, and every eye will see him."

Every eye. Not some eyes. Not the eyes of believers. Not just the people who were watching for him. Every single human being on the planet will witness this moment.

The atheist will see him. The agnostic will see him. The Muslim, the Hindu, the Buddhist, the witch, the satanist, the CEO, the homeless man, the president, the prisoner. Every eye.

There will be no debate about whether it happened. No fake news. No alternative explanations. No panel of experts offering naturalistic theories. No government cover-up.

Every eye will see him.

And everyone will know exactly who he is.

**The King Appears**

Revelation 19:11-13. "Now I saw heaven opened, and behold, a white horse. And he who sat on him was called Faithful and True, and in righteousness he judges and makes war. His eyes were like a flame of fire, and on his head were many crowns. He had a name written that no one knew except himself. He was clothed with a robe dipped in blood, and his name is called The Word of God."

This is not the gentle Jesus of the Sunday school paintings.

This is not the meek and mild Savior holding a lamb.

This is not the long-haired hippie offering free hugs and good vibes.

This is a warrior king.

His eyes are fire. Literal fire. Flames where pupils should be. The kind of gaze that sees through walls, through skin, through bone, through every lie you've ever told yourself. Nothing hidden. Nothing concealed. Every secret exposed in the light of those burning eyes.

On his head, many crowns. Not one crown. Many. Every crown ever worn by every king who ever lived is nothing compared to the authority resting on this head. He is King of kings. Lord of lords. The ruler of every nation, every throne, every power that ever existed or ever will exist.

His robe is dipped in blood. Not his own blood. Not this time. The blood of his enemies. The blood of those who made war against him. The blood of Armageddon.

And his name is The Word of God.

The same Word that said "Let there be light" and the universe exploded into existence.

The same Word that calmed the storm with three syllables.

The same Word that called Lazarus out of the grave.

That Word is now a sword. And it's coming for the rebellion.

### The Armies of Heaven

Revelation 19:14. "And the armies in heaven, clothed in fine linen, white and clean, followed him on white horses."

He doesn't come alone.

Behind him, stretching back beyond the limits of human vision, the armies of heaven ride. Angels. Millions of them. Billions. More angels than there are stars in the sky. More angels than there are grains of sand on every beach on earth.

And not just angels.

The saints. The great cloud of witnesses. Everyone who ever trusted in him, whoever believed the promise, whoever held on through persecution and martyrdom and suffering. They ride behind him now. Clothed in white. Seated on white horses. Finally seeing the victory they died believing in.

Abraham is there. Moses is there. David is there. Elijah, Isaiah, Jeremiah, Daniel. Peter, Paul, James, John. Every martyr. Every faithful believer from every century of human history.

They ride behind the King.

The ground trembles beneath the thunder of their approach. The air vibrates with the sound of hoofbeats that number in the trillions. The armies of heaven descending on a world that chose the wrong side.

### The Sword

Revelation 19:15. "Now out of his mouth goes a sharp sword that with it he should strike the nations."

He doesn't need weapons.

He doesn't need tanks or missiles or drones or nuclear warheads. He doesn't need generals or strategies or supply lines. He doesn't need anything the armies of earth rely on.

He has a sword. And it comes out of his mouth.

The same mouth that spoke creation into existence will speak destruction onto his enemies. One word. That's all it takes. The same voice that said "Let there be light" will say something else.

And it will be over.

Isaiah 11:4. "He shall strike the earth with the rod of his mouth, and with the breath of his lips he shall slay the wicked."

The breath of his lips. A whisper. An exhale. The most powerful militaries on earth, the mightiest weapons ever devised, the combined might of every nation foolish enough to stand against him...

Silenced by a single word.

## The Kings of the Earth

Not everyone will be celebrating.

Revelation 6:15-17. "And the kings of the earth, the great men, the rich men, the commanders, the mighty men, every slave and every free man, hid themselves in the caves and in the rocks of the mountains, and said to the mountains and rocks, 'Fall on us and hide us from the face of him who sits on the throne and from the wrath of the Lamb! For the great day of his wrath has come, and who is able to stand?'"

Read that list again.

Kings. The people who run nations. The presidents and prime ministers and dictators and monarchs.

Great men. The famous. The influential. The powerful.

Rich men. The billionaires. The CEOs. The ones who thought money could buy anything.

Commanders. The generals. The admirals. The men who controlled the most powerful armies on earth.

Mighty men. The strong. The elite. The special forces. The ones who thought they were invincible.

Every slave and every free man. Everyone else. No exceptions. No exemptions.

They run.

They don't fight. They don't negotiate. They don't try to spin it or explain it away or form a committee to study it. They run.

They hide in caves. They crawl into holes in the ground. They beg the mountains to fall on them. They plead with the rocks to crush them. They would rather be buried alive than face the one they rejected.

Think about that.

These are the people who mocked him. Who passed laws against him. Who cancelled anyone who spoke his name. Who called his followers bigots and haters and science-deniers. Who thought they were building a world where he wasn't needed.

Now they're screaming at rocks to kill them.

Because facing the Lamb is worse than death.

### The Winepress

Revelation 14:19-20. "So the angel thrust his sickle into the earth and gathered the vine of the earth and threw it into the great winepress of the wrath of God. And the winepress was trampled outside the city, and blood came out of the winepress, up to the horses' bridles, for one thousand six hundred furlongs."

Blood up to the horses' bridles.

For sixteen hundred furlongs. That's two hundred miles.

Two hundred miles of blood, four feet deep.

This is the battle of Armageddon. This is where the armies of the world gather to make war against the Lamb. Every tank. Every fighter jet. Every aircraft carrier. Every nuclear submarine. Every soldier from every nation that answered the beast's call.

They come to fight God.

They lose.

Revelation 19:17-18. "Then I saw an angel standing in the sun; and he cried with a loud voice, saying to all the birds that fly in the midst of heaven, 'Come and gather together for the supper of the great God, that you may eat the flesh of kings, the flesh of captains, the flesh of mighty men, the flesh of horses and of those who sit on them, and the flesh of all people, free and slave, both small and great.'"

The birds are summoned before the battle begins.

Read that again. Before the battle begins, God sends out invitations to the vultures. Come and feast. The meal is almost ready.

He already knows the outcome. The invitation goes out in advance. The table is set before a single shot is fired.

This isn't a battle.

It's a slaughter.

### The Beast and the False Prophet

Revelation 19:20. "Then the beast was captured, and with him the false prophet who worked signs in his presence, by which he deceived those who received the mark of the beast and those who worshiped his image. These two were cast alive into the lake of fire burning with brimstone."

The beast. The one who demanded worship. The one who controlled the economy. The one who made war against the saints for forty-two months. The one who seemed unstoppable.

Captured.

The false prophet. The one who performed miracles. The one who called fire down from heaven. The one who deceived the nations. The one who pointed the world toward the beast.

Captured.

No trial. No appeal. No lengthy legal process. No chance to explain or justify or make a deal.

Cast alive into the lake of fire.

Not killed first. Cast in alive. The first two residents of eternal judgment. Thrown in while still breathing. While still conscious. While still able to feel everything.

Their reign of terror over. Their deception finished. Their power stripped away in an instant.

### The Dragon Bound

Revelation 20:1-3. "Then I saw an angel coming down from heaven, having the key to the bottomless pit and a great chain in his hand. He laid hold of the dragon, that serpent of old, who is the Devil and Satan, and bound him for a thousand years; and he cast him into the bottomless pit, and shut him up, and set a seal on him, so that he should deceive the nations no more till the thousand years were finished."

Satan.

The adversary. The accuser. The father of lies. The serpent in the garden. The one who started all of this thousands of years ago with a single question: "Did God really say...?"

Chained.

Not by God himself. By an angel. A single angel with a key and a chain. One angel. That's all it takes to bind the being who thought he could overthrow the Most High.

For thousands of years, Satan has roamed the earth. Deceiving. Destroying. Devouring. Whispering lies into the ears of humanity. Turning hearts against their Creator. Building his kingdom of darkness one soul at a time.

Now he's in chains.

Thrown into the pit. Locked away. Sealed. A thousand years of silence. A thousand years where humanity finally gets to see what the world looks like without his influence. Without his lies. Without his temptations. Without the constant whisper of rebellion in their ears.

A thousand years of peace.

### Israel Looks Upon Him

Now we come to the moment the whole Bible has been building toward.

Zechariah 12:10. "And I will pour on the house of David and on the inhabitants of Jerusalem the Spirit of grace and supplication; then they will look on me whom they pierced. Yes, they will mourn for him as one mourns for his only son and grieve for him as one grieves for a firstborn."

They will look on me whom they pierced.

For two thousand years, the Jewish people have been waiting for their Messiah.

Praying for him. Three times a day, facing Jerusalem, asking God to send the promised one.

Longing for him. Through persecution and pogrom and Holocaust. Through exile and wandering and genocide. Holding on to the promise that one day, one day, the son of David would come.

Watching for him. Searching the scriptures. Debating the signs. Wondering if this generation would be the one.

And when he appears in the sky...they will see the scars.

The nail marks in his hands. The wound in his side. The evidence of what happened on a hill outside Jerusalem two thousand years ago.

And they will know.

The one they've been waiting for is the one their ancestors rejected.

The one they've been praying for is the one who already came.

The Messiah is Jesus. Yeshua. The same one.

They will mourn. Scripture says they will mourn like someone mourning their only son. Like someone grieving for their firstborn. The grief will be overwhelming. The weight of two thousand years of blindness lifting in a single moment.

"It was him. It was always him. And we missed it."

The mourning will be bitter. The realization crushing.

71

But it won't last.

Because this isn't a tragedy. This is a reunion.

**The Celebration**

Romans 11:26. "And so all Israel will be saved, as it is written: 'The Deliverer will come out of Zion, and he will turn away ungodliness from Jacob.'"

All Israel will be saved.

Not some. Not a remnant. Not a handful who figured it out early. All.

The blinders come off. The veil is lifted. The partial hardening that came upon Israel for the sake of the Gentiles is removed. The nation that carried the oracles of God for three thousand years finally recognizes the one those oracles pointed to.

And the mourning turns to joy.

Imagine Abraham. The father of the faith. The one who believed God when it made no sense to believe. The one who waited twenty-five years for a promised son and then was willing to sacrifice that son on a mountain.

He's there. Resurrected. Standing in the presence of the King. Watching his seed—singular, Christ—blessing all nations just as God promised four thousand years ago.

The covenant is fulfilled.

Imagine David. The shepherd king. The man after God's own heart. The one who wrote psalms about a throne that would last forever, about a son who would reign without end.

He's there. Watching his son—his Lord—take the throne that was promised. The throne of David restored. The kingdom of Israel eternal.

Imagine Moses. The deliverer. The one who led Israel out of Egypt. The one who saw the promised land from a distance but never entered.

He's there. Finally home. Watching the greater deliverer—the one he prophesied about—bring the ultimate exodus. Not from Egypt. From sin. From death. From the curse.

Imagine the tears of joy streaming down faces that spent lifetimes in prayer and fasting and hope.

He's here. He's finally here.

### The Two Sticks

Ezekiel 37:16-17. "As for you, son of man, take a stick for yourself and write on it: 'For Judah and for the children of Israel, his companions.' Then take another stick and write on it, 'For Joseph, the stick of Ephraim, and for all the house of Israel, his companions.' Then join them one to another for yourself into one stick, and they will become one in your hand."

For centuries, Israel was divided.

The northern kingdom. Ten tribes. Scattered by Assyria. Lost among the nations. Forgotten by history.

The southern kingdom. Judah and Benjamin. Exiled to Babylon. Returned. Scattered again by Rome. Wandering for two thousand years.

Two sticks. Two kingdoms. Two histories of suffering and exile and loss.

No more.

Ezekiel 37:22. "And I will make them one nation in the land, on the mountains of Israel; and one king shall be king over them all; they shall no longer be two nations, nor shall they ever be divided into two kingdoms again."

One nation. One king. Never divided again.

The lost tribes found. The scattered gathered. The divided made whole.

The promise to Abraham fulfilled. The covenant with David honored. The prophecies of the prophets accomplished. Every word. Every jot. Every tittle.

The twelve tribes reunited under the Son of David, ruling from Jerusalem, the city of the Great King.

This is what the whole Bible has been pointing to.

This is the ending that makes sense of everything that came before.

This is the happily ever after that isn't a fairy tale.

**The Kingdom**

What happens after the return?

Isaiah 2:4. "He shall judge between the nations and rebuke many people; they shall beat their swords into plowshares, and their spears into pruning hooks; nation shall not lift up sword against nation, neither shall they learn war anymore."

No more war.

Let that sink in. For all of human history, there has been war. Every generation. Every century. Every decade. Somewhere on this planet, people have been killing each other.

No more.

The weapons become farm tools. The tanks are melted down for tractors. The missiles are dismantled. The military academies close. The defense budgets disappear. The war memorials become relics of a forgotten age.

For the first time in human history, peace. Real peace. Global peace. Enforced by a King who cannot be defeated, cannot be corrupted, cannot be voted out of office, cannot be assassinated, cannot be overthrown.

Isaiah 11:6-9. "The wolf also shall dwell with the lamb, the leopard shall lie down with the young goat, the calf and the young lion and the fatling together; and a little child shall lead them. The cow and the bear shall graze; their young ones shall lie down together; and the lion shall eat straw like the ox. The nursing child shall play by the cobra's hole, and the weaned child shall put his hand in the viper's den. They shall not hurt nor destroy in all my holy mountain, for the earth shall be full of the knowledge of the Lord as the waters cover the sea."

Creation healed.

The curse reversed. The fall undone. The animal kingdom transformed. Predators and prey lying down together. Lions eating straw. Wolves and lambs as companions. Children playing with cobras. Toddlers reaching into snake dens without fear.

The earth itself transformed into what it was always meant to be. What it was before sin entered. What it will be forever after sin is finally dealt with.

Isaiah 65:20. "No more shall an infant from there live but a few days, nor an old man who has not fulfilled his days; for the child shall die one hundred years old."

Lifespans extended.

A hundred years old and you're still considered a child. The effects of the fall rolled back. Death itself pushed to the margins. People living for centuries. Watching their great-great-great-grandchildren grow up. Building legacies that span generations.

Zechariah 14:9. "And the Lord shall be King over all the earth. In that day it shall be—'The Lord is one, and his name one."

One King. Over all the earth.

Not just Israel. Not just the Middle East. Not just the religious people. Every nation. Every tongue. Every tribe. Every people group. All under the rule of the one who proved his right to rule by dying for the very people he would govern.

The nations will stream to Jerusalem. Year after year. Generation after generation. They will come to learn his ways. They will bring their gifts and their worship. They will see the King in his glory.

And he will reign with justice and righteousness forever.

**The Pattern**

Step back for a moment.

Look at what we've traced through this book.

Jesus was born on a feast. Tabernacles. The feast of dwelling. God with us. Emmanuel.

He was circumcised on the eighth day. The day of new beginnings.

His ministry began on a feast. The Day of Atonement. The holiest day on the Hebrew calendar.

His first Passover confirmed the timeline. Forty-six years of temple construction. The conversation no one was meant to have. The detail that anchors everything.

He was crucified on a feast. Passover. The lamb slain. The blood applied. The death angel passing over.

He was buried before sundown. In the tomb for three days and three nights. Exactly as he promised. Exactly as Jonah foreshadowed.

He rose on a feast. First Fruits. The first one raised from the dead. The firstborn among many brethren.

Every single event in his first coming landed on its appointed feast.

You think his second coming will be any different?

### The Feast They Forgot

There's one feast we haven't talked about yet.

One feast that sits at the beginning of the fall festival season. One feast that has never been fulfilled. One feast that's been waiting for two thousand years for its moment.

The Feast of Trumpets.

Yom Teruah in Hebrew. The day of the awakening blast. The day the shofar sounds. The day the king is announced.

In ancient Israel, trumpets served three purposes. They gathered the people. They announced war. And they signaled the arrival of the king.

Paul writes in 1 Thessalonians 4:16, "For the Lord himself will descend from heaven with a shout, with the voice of an archangel, and with the trumpet of God."

Trumpet of God. Feast of Trumpets.

1 Corinthians 15:52 says, "In a moment, in the twinkling of an eye, at the last trumpet. For the trumpet will sound, and the dead will be raised incorruptible, and we shall be changed."

The last trumpet. The final blast of the shofar.

The Feast of Trumpets was always about the return of the King.

**The Day No Man Knows**

Remember Chapter 1?

Jesus said, "But about that day and hour no one knows, not even the angels of heaven, nor the son, but the father only."

For centuries, this verse has been used to shut down anyone who tried to understand the timing. "No man knows! Stop looking! It's arrogant to even try!"

But we showed you what that phrase actually meant.

The Feast of Trumpets is the only feast that falls on the first day of a Hebrew month. And Hebrew months begin with the new moon. But you can't calculate the new moon with perfect precision. You have to watch for it. Two witnesses had to spot the first sliver of the moon and report to the Sanhedrin. Only then could the feast be declared.

This created a 48-hour window of uncertainty. The feast would fall on one of two days, but no one knew exactly which one until the moon was sighted.

What did the Jews call this feast?

*The day no man knows.*

Jesus wasn't forbidding us from understanding the timing.

He was telling us which feast to watch for.

## The Convergence

Now watch what happens when you do the math.

We established that the abomination of desolation is set up on First Fruits 2027. Sunset March 27 to sunset March 28, 2027.

Daniel 12:11 says there are 1,290 days from the abomination to...something. Something significant. Something worth counting to.

Start from First Fruits March 27, 2027. Count forward 1,290 days.

You land on Yom Kippur 2030. The Day of Atonement. October 6-7, 2030.

But that's not all.

The two witnesses begin their ministry thirty days after the abomination. April 27th. They prophesy for 1,260 days.

Start from April 27, 2027. Count forward 1,260 days.

You land on Yom Kippur, October 6, 2030. The same day.

Two countdowns. Two different starting points. Two different lengths.

Same destination.

## The Days of Awe

In Jewish tradition, there's a period called the Yamim Noraim. The Days of Awe. The ten days between the Feast of Trumpets and Yom Kippur.

These are the most solemn days on the Hebrew calendar.

According to tradition, on the Feast of Trumpets, God opens the books. The Book of Life. The Book of Death. He begins to write names. To make judgments. To render verdicts.

But the books aren't sealed on Trumpets.

*They're sealed on Yom Kippur.*

The ten days in between are a final opportunity. A last chance to repent. A closing window to get right with God before judgment is final.

The gates of heaven are opened on Trumpets. They remain open through the Days of Awe. And they close ten days later at the end of Yom Kippur.

Once they close, judgment is sealed.

Do you see it?

## The King Returns

Messiah returns on the Feast of Trumpets.

The sky splits. The trumpet sounds. The King appears. Every eye sees him.

Israel looks upon him whom they pierced. They mourn. They recognize. They repent.

And then...ten days.

Ten days for the world to respond. Ten days for the nations to fall on their faces. Ten days for every human being on earth to make a choice.

The Days of Awe.

The final altar call in human history.

And then Yom Kippur arrives. The Day of Atonement. The 1,290 days complete. The 1,260 days complete. The punishment periods for Israel and Judah expire.

The books are sealed.

Judgment is final.

## The Date

Everything we've traced in this book points to the same window.

Herod died in 4 BC, which means Jesus was born in 5 BC. His birth on Tabernacles in 5 BC means his ministry began on the Day of Atonement in 26 CE. His ministry lasted three and a half years, which means he was crucified on Passover 30 CE. His resurrection on First Fruits 30 CE is where Daniel's clock paused.

Israel's punishment began in 701 BC. Multiply by seven for unrepentance. 2,730 years later brings you to 2030.

Judah's punishment began in 70 CE. Multiply by seven. Then seven again. 1,960 years later brings you to 2030.

The abomination of desolation occurs on First Fruits 2027. Add 1,290 days. You land on Yom Kippur 2030.

The two witnesses begin thirty days later. Add 1,260 days. You land on Yom Kippur 2030.

Yom Kippur 2030 is when the books are sealed. When judgment is final. When the punishment periods expire. When Daniel's 70th week is complete.

And ten days before Yom Kippur...

Is the Feast of Trumpets.

*The day no man knows.*

The day the sky splits. The day the trumpet sounds. The day every eye sees him.

September 27, 2030.

That's the date.

Not a guess. Not a speculation. Not wishful thinking or newspaper exegesis or someone picking a year and hoping the numbers work.

Every timeline converges. Every calculation confirms.

Every feast alignment points to the same moment.

The Feast of Trumpets. September 27, 2030.

*The King returns.*

YOU JUST SAW THE ENDING.

Now carry it with you.

I built The Timeline — a single printable page with every date, every calculation, and every prophetic clock from this book. From 701 BC to Hanukkah 2030. One page. The entire roadmap.

Stick it on your refrigerator. Bring it to church. Hand it to everyone you love. Because when the abomination of desolation appears on First Fruits 2027, this page becomes the most important piece of paper in your house.

Here's what you do:

1. Go to ShittyToHappy.com/timeline

2. Enter your email address

3. Hit the button

4. The Timeline downloads instantly — no password, no nonsense

That's all I need from you — your email. In return you get a front-row seat to the most important countdown in human history.

I'll also keep you in the loop on new content, podcast appearances, and updates to the prophetic timeline as events unfold.

ShittyToHappy.com/timeline

The clock is ticking. Are you watching?

The 2030 Prophecy

# About the Author

I spent over 1,000 hours fact-checking the Messiah 2030 YouTube video series using primary historical sources—Josephus, the Talmud, Eusebius, and the original Hebrew and Greek texts. What I found confirmed everything in those videos and then some.

I'm not a seminary graduate. I'm a SAG actor with over forty-five years in the business. I starred in a television series with Michelle Pfeiffer called *B.A.D. Cats,* played Daisy Duke's boyfriend on *Dukes of Hazzard,* and appeared in the hit film *Jesus Revolution.* I've spoken on stages all over the United States and spent decades in the seminar business.

But my real education came from thirty-plus years studying Hebrew and Greek under Dr. Roy Blizzard, one of the foremost scholars of biblical languages in the United States. That training taught me one thing: never trust a translation when you can read the original.

This book is what happens when you let the math speak for itself.

You can visit me at ShittyToHappy.com

To contact the author, send an email to:
info@ShittyToHappy.com

The 2030 Prophecy

# Other Books by Steve Hanks

*HELL NO! The Great Heist*

If *The 2030 Prophecy* showed you when he's coming back, *Hell No! The Great Heist* shows you what he's coming back to fix.

For 1,500 years, the church has taught that God tortures the majority of humanity in conscious fire for all eternity. *Hell No!* dismantles that doctrine word by word using the original Greek and Hebrew texts. What you'll discover is that the God of the bible isn't a cosmic torturer. He's a divine surgeon. And the fire isn't punishment. It's purification.

Every mistranslated word. Every theological hijacking. Every proof text that collapses under its own weight when you read it in the original language.

Available on Amazon.

## Shitty to Happy Trilogy

**Book One:** *Shitty to Happy in 21 Minutes: THE SECRET KINGDOM*

An accidental discovery smacked me in the face back in 1983. It was a ridiculously simple method to force-feed peace and happiness into your heart. This method is so powerfully overwhelming that even if for some strange reason you didn't want to be happy, you can't stop its power. When you detonate this explosive God-given power, your body and heart have no other choice but to submit to this power to catapult you onto the path to happiness.

Available on Amazon.

**Book Two:** *Shitty to Happy in 21 Minutes THE EVIL QUEEN*

For 2,000 years, the church has been hunting the devil in the wrong zip code. Jesus gave us the address in Mark 7 — the human heart. Not some red-horned boogeyman on a pitchfork. A voice. The one that whispers the affair, suggests the lie, justifies the revenge. She sounds exactly like you because she's been rehearsing your whole life.

THE EVIL QUEEN dismantles the mythology of Satan as a third-party cosmic villain and exposes what the Hebrew text has said all along: the *yetzer hara* — the evil inclination — is the human heart gone rogue. Murder, lust, greed, deceit, pride? Jesus said every last one of them proceeds from within. No devil required.

The call is coming from inside the house. This book tells you who's on the line.

All titles available in paperback and eBook on Amazon.

All audiobooks available at TheSecretKingdom.org

www.ingramcontent.com/pod-product-compliance
Lightning Source LLC
Chambersburg PA
CBHW072208090426

42740CB00012B/2441